THE FATES WILL HARMONIZE FOR YOU

A COLLECTION OF POSITIVE & UPLIFTING
POETIC AFFIRMATIONS WRITTEN & ARRANGED
BY RH FOWLER

This collection

Of verse

Is dedicated to

You.

I hope this motivates

You.

I hope this

Inspires

You

In some way.

THE FATES WILL HARMONIZE FOR YOU

A COLLECTION OF POSITIVE & UPLIFTING POETIC AFFIRMATIONS WRITTEN & ARRANGED BY RH FOWLER

WRITTEN BY RH FOWLER

EDITED BY JD WALLACE

I enjoy

The life

I was given.

There is no other

Person

I would rather

Be

Than me.

My worth

Will not

Be calculated

By others,

I define

My own

Sense of self,

And nobody else

Has a say.

I will keep

Pushing through the dark,

For I know

Daybreak

Will meet me

Soon.

My life

Matters

To so many

People,

And so does

My health

And wellbeing.

There are people

That care

About me

And they are

There

If I need them.

I will

Silence

The fear

I have

For change

With a hopeful

Optimism

That will rub off

On everyone

Who encounters

It.

The days

Are long

Enough,

It is time

To spend

My hours

Wisely.

Time to

Start going

For my goals

Instead of excusing

Myself

From the chase.

Every day

Is a new

Set of

Challenges,

And I will

Meet each one

With a smile,

And open arms.

I do not

Need pity,

I am a warrior,

And I can comfort

Myself

In distress.

I do not

Expect

A helping hand,

I appreciate them,

But I am

Independent,

I am

My own

Person,

Capable

Of changing

This very

World.

Change is

Nothing,

I will

Adapt

To any

Adversity

And thrive.

I will

Keep my

Head

In rough

Situations.

I will be

The pillar

Of calm

That others

Look to

For strength.

I am

Here,

In this moment,

And nothing

In the entirety

Of existence

Can break

My deep

Focus.

Every

Bad

Choice

That I make

Only helps

To strengthen

My future self,

Who will

Avoid

Such costly

Errors.

My life

Will continue

To get better

Because

I am putting

The necessary

Work

Into that

Dream.

I am

Smart,

I am

Funny,

And

I am

In control.

I create

My mood,

And the way

That I feel.

I do not

Need

To make

A show

Of my intelligence,

I know

How smart

I truly am.

Words

Only mean

What I let them

Mean.

I am the

Only one

Who can get under

My skin.

My

Love

Is truly

A one of a kind

Energy

That can

Help

Heal

The entire

World.

My life

Is on

A good

Path.

I am

Incredibly

Satisfied

With my

Decision making.

Be yourself,

Always.

Never waver,

My darling,

For you are

An incredible

Force

That people

Will love

If you simply

Let them.

I will always

Do my best

In any situation.

I am

Adaptable,

I am

Strong,

I am

Brave enough

To see any

Difficulty

Through.

I am

A bold

Masterpiece,

I am

A work of

Art

That deserves

Love

And

Adoration.

I will

Love

Myself

Under

Any

And

All

Circumstances.

Failure

Does not

Bother me,

I brush it off,

Because I am

Ambitious,

Because I am

Always reaching

For the stars.

I will

Radiate

Love

And

Peace,

Especially

When the

Energies

Of

Hate

And malice

Abound.

I won't

Hate myself

For not

Being

Universally

Loved.

You can't

Please

Everyone,

And I will

No longer

Care to.

I will

Soar

In this life.

I can

Already

Feel

The air

Beneath

My wings.

I will

Live out

The life

I want,

Putting my

Interests first.

I will no longer

Conform

To some pre—ordained

Path,

My existence

Is something

I own.

I know

How

Talented

I am,

And I will

Work

Hard

To let

The world

Know.

I am

Doing

Just fine.

I am

Living

Life

At my own

Speed,

And that

Speed

Works well

For me.

I have

Standards,

And I will

Never

Ever

Compromise

Them

Because of

Expediency

Or easiness.

I hold

Myself

In very

High

Esteem.

People

Want

To be my friend,

People

Want

My opinion on things.

There is

No goal

Too big

For me to reach,

So long as I

Have

A plan

To get there.

I will always try to be

Prepared

For the challenges

I undertake.

Love

And

Good vibes

Will pour

From me

This day.

Negativity

Will have

No choice

But to cheer up

When it sees me.

I will

Always be

Honest,

And I will always

Tell those

I care for

How I feel,

For hiding

Emotion

Is selfish,

And will only

Hurt everyone

In the end.

I will

No longer

Entertain

Situations

That are not

Conducive

To my growth

As a human.

I am far too old

And far too wise

To fall into

That trap

Anymore.

I love

Myself,

This is true,

And I will

Help others

Love

Themselves

Too.

There is

Nothing more

I can do

Than give

My best effort.

Then,

Even if I lose out,

Even if I fail,

I can rest easy

Knowing

That I gave it

Everything.

I know

Myself

When many

People

Have no idea

Who they are.

This is my

Strength,

This is my

Place of power.

I will find

A way

To express myself

That moves

My soul.

And I will

Lose the world's

Expectations

And gain

A deeper understanding

Of myself

Through that

Process.

Giving up

Is never

In the cards

For me.

Never.

I am no quitter,

I finish what

I set out

To do,

Even if

The results

Aren't in my favor.

Ambition

Is one

Of my

Great allies.

We are fond

Of each other,

And very well

Acquainted.

I know

Victory

And

Defeat

Very well.

They motivate me

To do my best,

And whatever

The outcome may be,

I greet both

Warmly.

I am

A

Blinding

Beacon

Of

Blessings.

My

Soul

Is an

Instrument

For

Good.

I know

What

I need to do

To succeed.

And, with my

Faith in myself,

And the universe,

I know

I will do

Great things.

Obstacles

Are

Nothing.

The only

Thing they can

Do to me

Is teach me.

I am

The master

Of my own

Fate.

So, with that

In mind,

I will

Steer my life

In the direction

That I choose.

I am

A loving,

And caring

Person.

I was raised

With values,

And I am

Compassionate

Toward all

Mankind.

I will

Chase

The

Things

My heart

Dreams of,

And

I will

Meet

My desires

Face to face

In reality.

If the

Path is

Treacherous

Then I know

That the

Reward

Will be

Extraordinary.

So, I must

Keep going.

I must

Keep pushing

Onward.

I have

The utmost

Faith

In my

Intuition

And

Instincts.

They will surely guide me

To where I want

To be.

I

Love

My body,

I

Love

My soul,

I

Love

Myself

As a

Completed

Whole.

I have lost

Many, many

Times.

But,

Achieving

What you

Set out for

Is always worth

That prospect of defeat.

And with this in mind,

I never despair,

For I know that victory

Will be beautiful.

I

Will

Thoroughly

Enjoy

My life.

Today is

Mine,

And I will

Love

Every

Waking second

That I'm afforded.

I am

Important,

And I

Am

Loved.

There is no need

To feel

Lonely,

For my existence

Is one

Of incredibly

Vast beauty.

I am

My

Own

Biggest

Fan.

It is important

That I believe

In what I am doing,

And that

I cheer

Myself on.

There

Is absolutely,

Positively

Nothing

That

Life

Can throw

At me

That I

Cannot handle.

I will be strong,

I will see it all

Through.

I

Have

A vibrant

Personality,

And I will not

Be afraid

To be my true,

Funny

Self

Around

Anyone.

I

Will not

Be afraid

To reward

Myself

For hard work.

I will accept

When I do

A good job,

And I

Will not be

So

Self-critical.

I will

Work on

The things

I can

Improve,

And I will

Be bold enough

To forgive myself

For being human.

For having faults.

I will

Learn,

And I will

Be perceptive.

I know that

I do not

Know

Everything,

So I am

Hungry

For knowledge

And wisdom.

My talents

Will open

Doors

That lead to tremendous

Opportunity.

I must

Remember

That the

People

Who hate me,

Usually don't really

Hate me,

They loathe

My success.

My

Friendship

And

Attention

Are gifts,

And I will

Give them

To the

Deserving.

I will

Heal.

Then, I will jump

Over this hurdle,

And sprint

Quicker than ever

Before.

I can improve

My life.

I can improve

The way

That I relate to

This world

And its miraculous

Inhabitants.

All I need to do

Is figure out

My calling,

And the rest

Will follow.

A good routine

Leads to

A good balance

In life.

I will find what works

For me,

I will find what works

For my soul.

I accept what

Is past,

And all of the things

About me

That I cannot change.

In this

I am fine,

In this,

I have found peace.

Happiness and wealth

Are merely mind-states.

I am happy because I live,

I am wealthy because I have

Deep relationships.

The powers of

The universe

Will guide me

To where I need to be.

I am walking on the path

To success,

Dust just covers

The road.

I will love

With my complete heart,

And my complete soul.

And I will expect

Absolutely nothing

In return.

I choose

To let go,

I choose

To cast off

The weight

Of the past

So that I may soar

Triumphantly

Into my future.

Every day

Is a lesson,

And every waking moment,

An opportunity

To learn.

I am capable of doing

Incredible things.

I will

Achieve

Greatness

In my pursuits.

The fates

Will indeed harmonize

For me

One day.

I can almost hear their

Beautiful song

Echoing

In my mind.

The past has left.

It means nothing now,

And the future has not

Happened yet.

There is only

This very

Moment,

And I will own

This space

And fill it

With the focus

It deserves.

I will spread

Love and joy

To all those

Who are in need,

Because I know

How nice it is

To have someone

Remind me

That these concepts

Exist,

Especially when I feel

That they are lacking

In my life.

The ground may quake,

And shake my foundation,

But I am a pillar of

Tranquility,

A universe of

Calm

In my own right.

I will adapt

To the curveballs

This life throws my way,

For I am a fighter,

And there is nothing but

Heart

Invested in

Everything that I do.

Positive

Energy

Creates

Positive

Thinking.

I will surround

Myself

With the good

In my life,

And I will

Understand,

And avoid

The bad.

I can change this.

With a little focus,

With a little will-power,

I can become

What I set out

To be.

I am beautiful,

And I must not

Be afraid

To let the entirety

Of this world know.

I take care of myself

And I celebrate

The glorious flaws

That make me,

Me.

I will no longer

Succumb

To my fears

Or neuroses,

I will let the

Boldness of my

Beating heart

Be my guide,

And if it ends badly,

That romantic muscle

Will have been satisfied

All the more.

Every second

I am alive

Is a blessing,

An opportunity

To live

And to be privileged

With life

On this earth.

I have already won

The lottery.

I have the

Courage

To admit

When I am

Wrong.

I also have the

Intelligence

To understand

Why.

I will admire

The good things

About myself.

I will love

My talents and gifts,

And I will

Share them with

The whole

World.

I am giving

My time

And focus

To something

Far bigger

Than myself.

And, one day,

All of that dedication

Will pay off.

I can already see

The finish-line,

And the crowd

Screaming my name.

The universe

Gave me

A great opportunity

Called "life,"

And I will make the

Most

Of it.

it is indeed

A rarity,

And a great blessing

After all.

I will strive

For better

Health,

But I will not

Beat myself down

For slipping up

From time to time.

I am human,

And I am

Not perfect

After all.

Negativity

Will not affect me

In any

Way, shape, or form.

If it does, it is because

I let it,

And I will simply

Not let

The bad energies

Win.

New days

Are a blessing.

I am alive and well,

And I have

Another twenty-four hours

To spread love and light

To all.

My smile

Makes others

Smile.

It is important

To spread that

Love and cheer

Today,

And every day

That I can.

I control

This moment.

The past and future

Hold no weight

Here,

They do not matter.

In this space,

I will take life

One second

At

A

Time.

I will root for

My dearest

And closest

Of friends

To succeed.

Because, when they do,

That positive energy

Comes back

To our circle,

And it inspires

The whole group

To achieve great things.

My heart

And mind

Will be open

To everyone.

I will show respect

For different views,

And I will love my brothers

And sisters

In this human experience

All the same.

I will be bold.

I will not be afraid

Of work,

And failure,

Because failure

Is just a stepping stone,

Just a brick in the road

On the journey to

Success.

And this, my dear,

Is a journey

That I will not

Walk away from.

Be good to yourself.

That way,

The world

At large

Will know

Outright

To be good to you.

It all starts

With self-respect.

Take great pride

In who you are, my beloved,

For you are

A unique treasure.

I will not be

Afraid

To make my own way.

I will

Ignore the critics,

And I will

Ignore the hate.

I am aware

That my goals

Will take time to manifest,

But when they do,

I will claim

A magnificent bounty.

Quit setting

These distant goals

For yourself

And start appreciating

Who and where you are

Right now.

Walk out

Of the door

Ready to live

The life

You wish

To live

Starting today.

I will work

To spread love

Because someone needs to.

There is a tremendous

Lack of care

In this brutal world,

But I will help

My brothers and sisters,

My friends and my family

On this earth,

And we will

Move forward together,

In love, and united as one.

I know it takes

Time

To get better,

And I will work

Hard,

Day by day,

Until I am

Where I want

To be.

Pray for those

That yearn

For your downfall.

For their pain

Is deep,

And they could

Use

The well wishes.

You are

Something

More than

Special,

You're a

Miracle

In motion,

A one of a kind

Sort of

Love.

The people

I love

Are with me,

In my heart.

And because of this,

I am never

Truly alone.

I will give myself

Room

To be sad,

But I will know

When I need

To move on

From that space.

I will confront

Life

One challenge

At a time.

There is

No reason for me

To plan out

My entire future

Today.

I will rest

When it's time.

If I don't,

I am only

Hurting

My cause.

My goals

Deserve

My best,

My goals

Deserve

My all.

Treat yourself

To loving gestures,

Find time

To celebrate

The miracle

That is

You.

I will love

The people

Who show love

To me,

And I will wish

Nothing but the best

For those that don't.

There is no need

To spread any more

Ill—will.

I will spread love,

I will show love

To all.

I shall

Be a force of

Change,

I can, and will

Make a difference

In this incredible

World.

I will know

When to

Apologize,

And I will know

When to

Stop saying,

"I'm sorry."

Bad days

Will come,

But so will

Joyous

Days.

And these,

My love,

Are worth

All of the pain

That this world

Can muster.

It is okay

To let yourself

Crumble,

But do your

Best

To be brave,

And pick yourself

Up

From the

Wreckage

After the

Fall.

I will

Succeed

And live out

My dreams,

The drive

Within me

Is rare

Indeed.

I will

Help

Those

Who have

Given their

All

For the greater

Good.

I will love

The kind souls

Who would

Risk everything

For me.

I will continue

To try,

And to try

My hardest,

Against all odds.

I am a warrior,

And I will not

Be defeated

Easily.

I will survive

This darkness

And see my way

To the light

Of day.

I will not

Be easily

Swayed.

I am a rock,

A calm,

Collected

Space,

And I am

At peace

With everything

In my world.

My existence

Is filled with bliss

And great joy.

I am moved

By the beauty

Of my life,

And I deeply cherish

Every moment

That I am given

On this earth.

Our fates

Are in our own

Hands.

We were

Given an opportunity

To exist,

Now we must

Make the most

Of this blessing.

Chaos is good

Sometimes,

For it helps us

Appreciate

When waters

Are calm.

I am

A joy

To be around.

I love my

Friends and my family,

And they

Love

Me

Deeply

As well.

The time

To worry

About

Change

Is never.

Live in

The moment,

Adapt to the

Changes

And flows

Of life.

I am a

Conduit

For success

And good

Energies,

And I will embrace

The wave

Of positivity

That this

Brings.

This life

Never gives me

Any problem

That I cannot

Handle.

I am a universe

Of strength.

I am

Steadfast

And mighty.

This life is

A marathon,

And I intend

To finish it

With my peers,

Hand in hand,

the crowd

Roaring

For us all.

I author a

New book

Every day.

Each dawning

Sun

Is a chance

To write

A masterpiece.

I'm letting go

Of the weight

Of bad relationships,

And I am making room

For new love

To grow

In my heart

Like a beautiful

Flower.

When days are bad,

I look to powers

Greater than myself

For guidance,

And I find solace

In the fact

That everything

Happens for

A reason.

So, with this in my mind,

And in my heart,

I know that I will

Make it through.

The earth

Is a better place

Because

I am

On it.

I love

My reality,

And my relationship

With this world.

I will learn

To love

Myself

More.

Day by day

My reverence for

Me

Will grow.

I will set

Goals

For each day

That I know

Without doubt

Are achievable,

And through this

I will inch my way

Toward greatness.

This life

And all

Of its joy

Was meant

For me.

The mood

That I cultivate

Becomes

The vibe

That I put out

Into the world.

I will radiate

Peace and light

For others

To see,

So that their

Path

Through this

Life

May be

Bright

As well.

My good

Attitude

Will open up

Doors

That lead to

Great

Opportunity.

I am a

Star.

And when

It gets

Dark,

My shine

Will only

Brighten.

You are

Amazing,

And those who

Disagree

Simply do not

Understand

That simple

Truth.

It is within me

To make

Something

Great

By myself,

From nothing.

Many have done it,

Many will do it again,

And there is no difference

Between us

Except for

The motivation

To succeed.

I am in control

Of what I

Spend my

Time

Dwelling on.

Trivial thoughts

Will not make it

Through

The fortress walls

Of my mind.

I will no longer

Waste time

On those

Who won't

Even spare

A second

For me.

It will

Take

Tremendous

Amounts

Of work,

Sweat, tears,

And everything

In—between,

But I will

Triumph.

I will succeed

In what I set out

To do.

This

Moment

Right now

Is all I need

To be

Happy,

And at

Peace.

Each day

Is a tiny

Success

That will

Snowball

Into a giant

Avalanche

Of victory.

I am

More than

Worthy

Of the rewards

My work ethic

Will bring.

I feel

Good.

My health

Is in my hands,

And that is fine,

For I treat

My body

Like the temple

That it is.

My body

May break,

But I will

Rejuvenate,

And be

A better,

Stronger

Me.

I never worry

About needless

Conflict

Because

I plant

The seeds

Of peace

Wherever

I go.

I will respond

To all situations

With calm

And love,

Even when

I feel

Anger

And

Frustration

Nagging

At me.

All is

Well

In this

Moment,

In this space,

And I am

Immensely

Grateful

For this.

I observe

And address

My anger

And sadness

Without letting

Them steer

Or control

My thoughts.

I am at

Peace

With my life

And all

That is happening

Within it.

My resilience

Is no surprise,

I am granite,

I am as solid

And as sturdy

As a rock,

And I will

Let the world

Know this.

I choose

To live

In a

Mind-state

Of peace

And serenity.

My calm mood

Will help

Others

Find peace,

And the world

Will be better

Because of it.

I am

At ease.

Every inch

Of my body

Is calm,

Including

My mind.

I will only

Look to

The past

For wisdom,

Not for

Dwelling

On what

Could have

Been.

I will

Never

Settle,

My standards

Are high

Because I

Am deserving

Of greatness

In my life.

I will cause

A wave

Of love

And peace to

Wash over

My world,

And the universe

At large.

I will

Not be consumed

By thought,

And I will

Keep myself

In the moment

This day.

There

Will be times of

Great sadness,

But they will remind us

All

Of the immense beauty

Within our own

Existence,

And of all of the love

We have experienced

On this amazing

Journey.

Joy

Is my

Companion

And

Peace

Is my

Foundation.

I am

A fountain

Of light

That dazzles

All

With my good nature.

There is

Nothing

That I cannot

Comprehend.

The only

Factor

Is my

Interest

In the subject.

I am my own

Master,

And I choose

What I excel at.

I choose

What I

Spend

My precious

Time

And

Energy

Pursuing.

Nobody can

Force me

To do anything

That I do not

Want to do.

I can

Truly

Help

Others

If I try.

And that,

My dear,

Is a beautiful

Thing.

It may

Take a while,

But I will rebuild

My heart

From this

Brokenness.

The universe

Loves me

And has

Bigger, and better

Moments

In store

For my future.

Every instance

Of pain

Will lead me

To moments

Of greater

Joy

In the end.

I am

Cherished,

Even if I

Don't feel like I am

Sometimes.

I matter,

And there are people

That love me

Dearly,

And I love them

Dearly

As well.

If a problem

Finds me,

I will act

With a full

Heart,

And I will

Ease anger

Out of my

Mind.

Relationships

Will come

And go,

And I will

Not let them

Rule me.

I am happy

By myself,

My contentment

And peace

Does not rely

On others.

I will

Hold on

To some of

My love

For

Myself

This time.

If I fail,

I need to

Try again.

No quitting,

Ever,

No giving in.

I will rise above,

And I will

Eventually

Overcome

My struggles.

I will be

Successful,

And beyond all,

I will find

Joy on my path

To that place,

Doing the work

That I want

To do.

I have the

Power

Within me

To reinvent

My life

Whenever

I choose.

If I

Think

That I

Deserve

Better,

It is because

I more than likely

Do.

I deserve

The best

That this life

Has to offer,

And nothing less.

I will

No longer

Hold my mind

Hostage

With negative

Thoughts,

I will let them

Float on by,

Like water

Whipping

Down a stream.

If the

Hard work

Is there,

The results

Will be

As well.

My good

Fortune

Is no surprise

Because I

Work for it

Every single day.

I trust in

My heart,

And though it

May be wrong

At times,

It is my own,

And I relish every

Chance to learn

That it brings me.

There is

Magic

In the everyday.

In fact,

My whole world

Is supernatural,

Like something from a

Dream,

And there is

Nothing I can't

Imagine

Or achieve.

Love

Will be

The concept

That I dedicate

This day

To.

Hate will

Never find me

Because we

Live

On two separate

Worlds.

I am ready

For challenge,

And I am

Ready to

Explore

What is

Outside

Of my

Comfort zone.

There are

Things,

And thoughts

That I should

Simply

Let go of,

And I

Will

Let

Them

Drift

Away

With time.

Consistency

Certainly is

Key.

I need to

Maintain momentum,

I need to

Stick to my game-plan.

I respect

My abilities

And have

Faith

In the ventures

That I invest

My efforts into.

Things won't

Always

Work out

In your favor,

But that doesn't mean

That they

Will not

Work out

Later.

I will

Try my

Very best,

And I will run

Through the night,

Until I

See the

Finish line

In sight.

I brush off

What hate

I don't still

Feel pity

For.

I can pray

For good fortune,

But in the

End,

I was given

Every tool

Necessary

To succeed

At my birth.

I will do

This.

I am in

Command

Of my

Life

And my

Destiny

In this moment.

I see

My competition,

And I know

I can push farther

Than them.

This is my

Time

In the sun,

My moment

To shine.

I will be

Mindful

Of the

Double-edged

Swords

That can

Be forged

From my words,

And I will

Think

Before I speak.

I will always

Bring

A nuanced perspective

To any work that I do,

And I will always be

Proactive

About completing

The task at hand.

Some days

Are rough waves

That will try to

Drown you.

But you must fight

For that breath,

My darling,

You must fight

Until you

Feel the air

In your lungs

Once more.

I will

Pick myself

Up

Piece–by–piece

From the rubble

Until I am

A new

Sort of

Whole.

My dreams

Will stay but

Dreams

If I don't work

To make them real,

So I must

Truly push myself

To get what I want.

I must dedicate myself

To my cause.

A masterpiece

Of any kind

Isn't created

In just a day,

And I have

To realize that.

Slow progress

Is better than

No progress,

After all,

So I will take my time,

And I will enjoy

This ride.

My greatness

Will manifest

When

And

Where

It needs to.

Patience

Is truly

The most

Mighty

Of allies.

I know that

The road

To success

Will be long,

So I'll keep my

Head up,

Humming a song.

No matter

The cause

Of my woe

Or my dread,

I will do my best

To put my anger

To bed.

Time

Is oh–so

Valuable,

And mine

Cannot

And will not

Be wasted.

I won't be

Afraid to

Boldly

Go.

I have

What it

Takes

To be an

Innovator,

To be a

Pioneer

In the field

Of my choosing.

I will

Trust

In my

Good qualities

To win the

Hearts and minds

Of my peers.

I do not need

A flashy gimmick

To gain approval,

My authentic-self

Is more than enough.

I won't let

Negative

Perceptions

Of me

Become my

Own perception

Of myself.

I deserve

A love

On my terms.

No more

Waiting

For things

To come to me,

I am going

For the gold

In my romantic endeavors,

And I will find

My true soulmate

One day.

I will look

To nature

To still my

Mind

In times

Of restlessness.

Mother Earth will

Guide me

To serenity.

I will

Note

The beauty

And splendor

In the natural world,

And I will marvel

At the genius

Cityscapes

Made by humans.

This world is wondrous,

And I will enjoy all

That it has

To offer me.

My

Mistakes

Are

Truly

Some of my

Best

Friends.

I won't

Fail

Like in

The past,

Oh no,

I am far smarter,

I am far wiser

This time around,

And I am ready

To succeed.

I take my

Goals

A day

At a time,

And I keep

My priorities

Well

In line.

I have to

Be willing

To go

To the places

That make my heart

And mind

Run wild,

For these are

The places

That will help me

Grow

Into the person

I want to be.

I have

Accomplished

A great deal

In my short

Life,

And I have

Every right

To be proud

Of what I have

Done

So far.

I know

When

I

Need

Space.

I know

When

I need

To say

"No."

Good

Things

Will happen

When I work

To make

Them happen.

This is the truth,

This is the key

To unlocking

Everything

That I want

In this life.

I will

Touch

The sky

With my

Ambition,

And I will

Reach the

Stars

With my

Success.

Positivity

Flows

Through every

Inch

Of my

Being.

My good vibrations

Appeal

To everyone

That encounters

Them.

My goals

Terrify

Me,

And this

Is a good

Thing.

I will carry that

Feeling

Into my work,

And it will

Motivate me

To beat

Any odds.

I am

Human,

And deserve

To be

Treated

As such.

I deserve

To have

My feelings

Respected

And my voice

Deserves

To be heard.

Conversation

Is my

Comfort zone.

I am at ease

Talking

To other people,

And I should never feel

Intimidated

By any other person's

Words,

For they cannot

Hurt or harm

Me.

I won't

Let my

Troubles

Consume me

Anymore,

For I am bigger

Than any

One

Problem

In my

Life,

And I must

Realize this.

I know that

I

Understand

My worth,

But I must not

Be afraid

To show

Other people

That I am

Valuable

As well.

The chaos

In my life

Is all a product

Of my own

Actions.

This is

The moment

I get back

On track.

This is

The moment

I regain

Control.

The whole world

Will know

My name

One day.

I am great

At what I do,

And I will be

Recognized

As the best

In my field.

My horizons

Are endless,

My opportunities

Abound

In this life.

I will

Have

Hope,

But,

I will be

Absolutely ready

For any,

And every

Outcome.

I am

Diligent,

I am focused,

And I am

Going to be

The best

At what

I do.

There is

Too much

Life

In front of me

To focus

On the past

Behind me.

I will always

Act

For the greater good,

And treat people

Right,

Just like I should.

I won't be

Afraid

Of being

True to

Myself

In all aspects

Of my

Life.

I am

Smart,

I am

Gifted,

I understand

Ideas and concepts

That take

Other people

A long while

To grasp,

And because of this,

I know that I am

At an advantage.

I will be

Genuine,

And I will

Do things

Out of the

Goodness

Of my

Heart.

Positive

Thoughts

And

Actions

Beget

Unexpected

Rewards.

Be good

To be good,

And good things

Will undoubtedly

Happen

To you.

I do not

Care

What others

May think,

I know

Who

I am,

Without a

Shadow

Of a doubt

In my mind.

I know that

Anger

Is an

Easy

Trap

To fall

Into,

And I will be

Vigilant

In trying

To avoid

Being caught

In its snares.

I am

Zen,

I am

In charge

Of my

Own

Sense

Of

Calm.

Breathe in.

I have

The skills

To get

To the top

Of my trade,

I am my only

Obstacle

In that

Pursuit.

My goals

Are clear,

And will

Clearly

Manifest

So long

As my

Focus

Is true.

I will never

Give

Small issues

Priority

In my mind.

I am focused

On the bigger

Picture.

I will

Motivate

Others,

And I will

Welcome all

Competition

In my field,

Because adversity

Demands

My best,

And I always

Amaze myself

When under pressure.

248

I will

Help my peers

Succeed

By showing them

That I can succeed.

I want the very

Best

For my life,

And every day

I try my

Hardest

To live

That idea.

I was born

Of love

So I will

Plant

Love's seeds

Wherever

I go.

My mind

And body

Are fine-tuned

Machines,

And I treat them

With the utmost

Respect

And consideration.

I am

Choosing

Happiness

As my guide

Today.

I refuse

To give up.

I refuse

To give in.

I set my

Own standards.

I define

How I react

To life.

I will only

Find time

For happy

Thoughts

And

Good

Energies.

I will

Make

Myself

Proud.

I only

Have to

Impress

Me,

And nobody

Else.

I will

Master my

Craft.

Day–by–day,

I will get better

At what I do.

I will put in

The effort

To be great,

And it will be

No surprise

To me

When I succeed.

I can't change

How someone

Feels about me,

But I can change

How I feel

About them.

And that,

My love,

Is a beautiful truth

To stumble upon.

I am grateful

For every

Single

Mistake

I have ever made.

They have

Always been

My greatest teachers,

And they have

Always given me

More insight into myself

Than any victory

Ever could.

My values

Are strong,

And I truly

Believe in them

As my guiding

Lights

In this life.

Nothing will ever

Dim

Their glow.

The only

Person

That can

Make my

Existence

Better

Is me.

But I have

To really want it.

I have

To really want

Change

For my life.

The

Results

Of hard work

Are easy

To see,

But the effort

It takes

To be great

Will require

All of me.

My existence

Evolves

In beautiful ways

Every day

That I'm

Alive.

So, I never stay sad

For too long,

Because I know that

Something exciting,

And interesting

Is just around

The corner.

The relationships

That I

Have forged

Throughout my brief

Life

Are beautiful,

And I wouldn't trade

Them

For anything else

In the world.

I won't run

From negativity,

I will simply acknowledge it,

And let

The bad vibes

Pass me by.

I will

Accept others

Without hesitation,

Unless they

Give me great reason

Not to

Embrace them.

I am not

Closed-off,

I am open

To all.

I constantly

Strive

For good,

And my

Life

Reflects

That

Pursuit.

If my

Best effort

Isn't good enough,

Then I simply

Need to

Refocus,

And try

Harder.

I will bury

My challenges,

I will not

Let my challenges

Bury me.

Never quit.

Everything

You want

Is so close,

My love,

So go,

Reach out,

And take

What is

Rightfully

Yours.

There is no need

For me

To see myself

In competition

With anyone.

I am in my own

League,

I play the game

My own way.

I know where

My faith

And allegiances

Lie.

I will not

Be shaken

From that

Foundation.

I will be true

To me,

And all

That I am.

My life

Is full of

Beauty

And infinite

Possibilities.

I will create

Miracles

Today

If I so choose.

I will never

In my life

Give up

My ability

To dream.

I will no

Longer

Let my

Thoughts

Trap my

Mind

Into a

Corner,

I will fight my way

Out,

And I will find

Peace, and calm

Again.

I know

The best

Revenge

Is always success,

And success

Is what I

Shall achieve.

The non-believers

Will still exist,

But they will think twice

Before they doubt

So assuredly

Again.

I will

Prove

The naysayers

And their

Ilk

Wrong.

This is something

I promise

To myself,

And to the world.

I am capable

Of inventing

New things.

I am smart enough to see

Possibility

And innovation

In all that I touch.

This gift

Will serve me well

As we move faster

Into the future,

And I am ready for those

Moments to come.

I know

What calm is,

I know what peace is,

And I know

That I can

Recognize both

Of those

Friendly faces again

If I ever find myself

Adrift and lost

In a sea

Of my thoughts

And emotions.

I will never

Count myself

Out.

I will prevail,

And I will show

The doubters

How wrong

They truly

Are.

I will no

Longer

Accept

Being

Ignored.

I am

Worthy

Of explanation,

Worthy

Of being

Listened to

And appreciated.

My faults

Are my

Own

To

Own,

And I will

Wear them

All

With pride.

If I

Miss out

On any opportunity

In this life,

It is my own fault,

And nobody

Else's.

I must be prepared

To accept

My mistakes

And move forward

With renewed vigor.

I have

No room

For

Hate or malice

In my heart.

That space will be

Reserved

For love and joy

From now on.

If I fail,

I will not

Quit,

Because I cannot

Let adversary forces

Conquer me.

No, my love,

Don't you see?

It is

I

That will conquer

Adversity

With my victory.

My will

And constitution

Are as strong

As I

Make them.

No other human

Has that sort of

Control

Over me,

No other human

Can tell me

What I can

And cannot do.

If I have

To fight

The noise

To make

My voice

Count,

To have it heard,

Then I will

Relentlessly

Pursue the podium

Until

I have reached the

Masses.

I will

Never

Let another

Person's

Idea of me,

And what they think

I should be,

Become my

Idea of me.

I have my own life,

And I will live it

In the way

That I see fit.

I am

More committed

To meeting my goals

Than my

Competition is.

I work harder,

I deserve the

Glory,

And it will eventually

Come

To me.

I will

Turn my

Dreams

Into

Goals

That I

Will reach.

I love

Myself.

I truly do.

I love myself

For everything

That I am,

And it is

Absolutely

Freeing.

I will

See this hardship

To the end,

For glory

Is what

Awaits me

On the other side

Of this struggle.

The pain I feel

Only cuts

As deep

As I let it.

My mind is more

Than strong,

It is in fact

A fortress

Of focus

And calm,

And I never dwell

On sad thoughts

For long.

I will work

Toward building

Good

In my life,

And I won't be

Afraid

To cut off

What I deem

Toxic

And bad

Energies

In a moment's notice.

I am

Loved

By a great many

People,

And they

Appreciate

All that I try to do

For them.

It is a beautiful

Life

Indeed.

I will

Stop to

Smell the

Roses

More often,

And I will

Enjoy the simple

Things

That make life

Beautiful.

I only have

Twenty–four hours

In a day,

So I can't waste time

Being upset,

I must use

Each minute to

Grow

In a positive

Way.

I will

Help others.

I will help

My fellow man,

Because if

They succeed,

I do as well,

And so does

The world

At large.

I will focus my energies

On making a difference

In the world,

For the globe

Is far too big

To just concern myself

With my own

Minuscule problems,

I have the power

To affect change,

To make a difference

In the lives of others,

And I absolutely will.

If I don't struggle

For my goals,

Somebody else will,

And they will reap those

Rewards.

I will not

Settle for this.

I will not settle for

Thinking about

What could have been

If I had just

Believed in my cause

More.

I am

A magnet

For health,

Wealth,

And personal growth.

I only attract

The good,

And I do well

At shunning

The bad.

I marvel

At my

Intellect

And thoroughly

Enjoy

Being in

My own

Company.

I am a treasure

To have

In any

Conversation.

I lighten the mood

And take discussion

To new heights.

I will

Hold my

Tongue

And use my

Words

To build

Conversation.

I will not use them

To destroy discourse.

I will not use them

Just for the sake

Of arguing.

I am level-headed.

I think deeply

Before making

Any decision,

Because I know

They all have

Consequences

That impact me,

And the people

That I love most.

I will

Simply

Work harder.

There is no magic

To success,

And there will be

No doubts

About my greatness

When my time comes.

I will not

Be afraid

To help my

Heart

Find

What it

Needs.

My existence

Is a reason

To celebrate.

I am fortunate

To have lived.

I look into

The mirror

Each morning

And I am

Ecstatic

About

The reflection

I see.

I am, by far,

The best

Me

I can be.

Even when

Life makes me

Stumble,

I know

I will find my way

To balance

Again.

And, when I achieve

Equilibrium,

I will take off

Running

Toward my dreams

Once more.

I really

Want

This.

I could have

Taken the

Easy way out,

But I want this

With all

Of my

Soul,

And I will

Do my best

To make it so.

Love

And

Hate

From my

Fellow man

Are both

Equally

Motivating.

They both

Drive me

To want to

Succeed.

My

Resolve

And

Persistence

Will see

Me through

Even the

Most raging

And violent

Of storms.

I woke up

This morning

With an incredible

Support system

Made up of

Treasured relationships.

My life

Is magic,

My life

Is wondrous.

The harder

I work

At this life,

The more

I will

Achieve,

And the better

I will feel

When all

Is said

And done.

This universe

Loved me

Enough

To allow me

Life,

So I must

Do my best

To revere

Creation,

And I must be thankful

For this miracle

Of an existence.

I will be

Cool,

I will be

Calm,

I will not be

Anxious

About what

I am doing

Anymore.

I am totally

In control

Of how I feel.

I will focus

On the task

At hand,

And it will

Be done

With precision

And the utmost

Care.

Adversity

Is simply

A workout

For my mind.

And with every

Exercise,

I get a little bit

Stronger.

It is important

That I don't let

Any

One idea

Or any

One person

Consume my

Thoughts.

I need my focus

To help me

Grow,

Not to

Obsess.

I am not

Afraid

Of failure,

I am not

Deluded

In my pursuits.

I am driven,

And my effort

Will carry me

To the promised land.

I choose

To feel

Good

Today.

I will let

Positive vibes

Rule

My mood.

I will

Listen to

My heart

More,

And I won't

Be so cruel

And ignore it

Out of

Fear

Of anything.

I trust

In myself

And the universe,

And I know

Neither

Will let me

Down.

I appreciate

Hurt

Because

It reminds me

Of how great

True

Joy

Can be.

I won't let

Anger

Inconvenience me

Or

Shake my

Composure,

And I will do my

Best

To respond

To life's challenges

With grace

And humility

In mind.

I know

That I

Am primed

For greatness,

I just have to

Put in the work

And make my

Ambitions

Real.

I will

Only react

To life

With goodness

In my heart,

For I have

True

Adoration

For all of creation.

I take

Myself

Seriously.

And if

Others

Do not,

They will

Soon see

How foolish

They were

In overlooking

My talents.

I treat

Progress

Like it is

My flesh

And blood.

We are

Family.

I am

Making moves.

I am succeeding

At reaching

My short term

Goals

Which will

Propel me

To long term

Satisfaction.

I measure my success

In the long view.

Not how much

Can I accomplish

In a day,

But how much

Can I accomplish

Every day

For ten years?

I will be steady

And resolute.

I will see it

All the way through.

I will

Go

After

It.

I will

Embark on this

Journey,

And I will

Find

My kingdom

At this adventure's

End.

I don't

Need

Any

Special

Treatment.

I just need

A deadline

For my work,

And my

Persistence

Will drive me

Toward

Completion.

I will

Look

For goodness

In every place

That I can,

And I will

Make sure

That it has a seat

At the table

Of ideas

When I am

Around.

I am

Complete

On my

Own.

I do not

Need

Another

Person

To make me

Feel

Whole.

You reap

What you

Sow,

And I choose to sow

Positivity,

Knowing

That force

Will

Return

Back

To me

Tenfold.

I will

Always try

To do what's

Right,

With all of my

Heart,

And

With all of my

Might.

Words

Can be

Stabbing

Daggers,

Or they can

Help us humans

Build bridges

Faster.

I will

Be more mindful,

And I will

Respect

This planet

And everything

On it.

I love my life.

I am an incredible

Human.

There is no goal

Too big

Or mountain

Too tall,

For I

Am a

Go-getter,

And challenges

Only make me

Smile.

I am the

Best

Me

That I

Can be,

I treasure

My story,

In victory

Or defeat.

I will

Never

Second-guess

The timing

Of my life.

I will shine

When I am

Ready,

And I will

Most certainly

Be ready

For that day.

I will

Admire

My greatest

Qualities,

And I will be

My own

Biggest

Fan.

I will

Help

Others

Admire

Themselves.

I will

Help others

See how

Truly

Beautiful

They are.

I will

Love

Without

Hesitation

Today.

I will

Do my

Best

To focus

More

On

Me

And less

On

Them.

I am

My own

Center

Of peace.

I control

My mind

And how

I am affected

By this

Life.

My strength

And resolve

Are undeniable,

I am a pillar

Of stability

In turbulent times.

I have

A lot

Of work

To do

On myself,

And I am

Up to

The task

Of bettering

Me.

My heart

Is a powerful

Medium

For love

And light.

It defines

Me,

I know

I am good

Because of that magic,

And I would

Never change it

For the world.

I will

Navigate

Love's

Ocean

With reverence

For the

Unpredictability

Of Mother Nature.

I will

Always try

To react

With love

And

Grace

In mind,

Whether

The situation

Is good,

Or

Dire.

I will

Find

Strength

In pain,

And I will

Come out

Of the fire

Of hurt

Anew,

Ready for

Whatever else

Life

May throw at me.

I will struggle,

And things

Will hurt me

In this life.

But I am stronger

Than the

Pain

That will

Come.

I will

Carry on

And live

Well.

I do not know what

Tomorrow

May hold

For me,

And those

I love,

But I will

March forward,

And I will accept whatever

This beautiful

Existence

Has in store,

Good and bad.

This life

Will deal me

Great hurt,

And great

Joy

As well.

I will seek out

Both,

I will feel

It all.

I am

Not afraid

To let

Hurt

Change me

For the better.

I won't shy

Away

From adventure

In this life.

I will leave this world

With a story

Worth remembering.

Peaceful energies

Will find me

Because I have

Opened myself

Up to them.

I am fine

With losing,

And loss

In all hues,

And I will work

With those

Setbacks

Until I feel

Whole,

And joyful

Again.

I am a

Force

Of goodness.

This world

Is a better

Place

Because

I am here

To be in love

With it.

I will greet

All of the grief

I encounter

With a smile,

And a tender heart.

I will not

Be afraid

To let my

Heart

Bleed

For someone

Or something

That I love.

The trick will be

Learning

How to stop

The flow

When necessary.

I am not

My worst mistakes.

I am an accumulation

Of the lessons

They have all

Taught me.

There is no

Metaphorical mountain

That I cannot climb.

The work just

Has to be there

To do it.

The drive

Has to be there

To do it.

And the beauty is,

It is all up to me to act,

For I am the curator

Of my destiny.

I will go

The distance.

The sprinters

In this marathon race

Don't alarm me,

For I will overtake them

In due time.

I will not

Let myself

Get discouraged

For too long.

It is good to feel

The weight of life,

But I will not be

Crushed

Underneath it.

I will run longer,

And I will go the extra mile

For my dreams.

I will sleep

And wake up to the sounds

Of them calling my name.

For I am the personification

Of what it is

To be dedicated,

And I will

Turn my visions

Into reality

Before I am gone.

Get up,

Shake off

The dust

Of old battles,

And get to work

On your dreams.

Do not

Forget

To breathe,

My dear.

Breathe

If only for a

Moment –

Because in that

Moment,

The answer

May reveal

Itself.

True wisdom

Comes from

Living,

With letting yourself

Fail

Once in a while.

Embrace the fall,

My love,

But prepare

To rise.

This is your life,

Own

Every bit of it.

Tell yourself

How beautiful

You are.

We have to

Love

Our own

Being

Before

Others

Can.

Brace yourself

For pain,

But understand

That joy

Will find you

Again.

Such is life,

My darling,

Remember this

Fact

When existence

Gets you down.

THE END

Thank you

For reading

My collection

Of poetic affirmations.

I hope that you found

Something inspiring

In my words,

And I hope that

Love and light

Finds you

And keeps you

Forever.

I love you all.

Made in the USA
Middletown, DE
02 January 2018